D0870712

* * * * * * *

- A COMPLETE HOME TRAINING PROGRAM -

* * * * * * *

BOOK TWO

Covering:

INSIGHT

BEHAVIOR

MODIFICATION

MISCELLANEOUS DOG PROBLEMS

Published by:

ANIMAL OWNERS MOTIVATION PROGRAMS

An Institute - Specializing in Animal Training and Psychology
(A Division of Rojon Enterprises and School of Dog Obedience)

Edited by Dianne Allen
Illustrated by Joyce L. Bond

Animal Owners Motivation Programs
P. O. Box 16, Frankfort, Illinois 60423

ADAMS PRESS
CHICAGO

TRAINING A DOG TO LIVE IN YOUR HOME

Book Two:

Insight Behavior Modification

by

John D. Weiss

Hundreds of hours of work went into the writing and preparation of this book. It could not exist without the help and encouragement from one very special person. She is my motivator, critic, typist and best friend. I dedicate this finished product to my Lady - Lenore.

CONTENTS

It is safe to say, the biggest problem concerning a dog owner is communication. This is the sometimes frustrating inability you experience when trying to communicate a given message to your pet. The understanding of each other's wants and needs is extremely important. When there is a failure to communicate, you can bet problems will inevitably arise.

Unfortunately, this book does not contain a magic wand that you can wave in order to make your problems disappear. I wish I could furnish you with such a device, but since that is impossible, let's do the next best thing.

If you are now experiencing a given problem, it could have taken many, many hours of some improper training procedure of yours to help in causing it to form. It should come as no surprise when I say - it may take some time and effort on your part to change or modify the unwanted behavior.

There are two ends to a leash. In order to achieve complete success, both ends must be equally trained, not just the dog's end, but your end too. So let us start on your end first. Remember - your past mistakes may be part of the cause, but you and your knowledge are also the much sought after magic wand - YOU ARE THE CURE.

WHAT TYPE OF DOG DID YOU CHOOSE?

1. A DOG AN EMOTIONAL SYMBOL

Have you ever given any thought as to why a person obtains or even wants a dog? Simplified, you may hear these reasons from others: as a playmate for the kids, or as a watch dog, etc. All very true but if you look beyond the surface, beyond the obvious, you will see that a pet can be many things to many people, and yet, at the same time, be potentially, psychologically devastating!

A pet, especially a dog, is often an emotional symbol that can, and usually does, reflect and mirror back the most deeply ingrained individuality of the owner. The type of breed that is chosen may often be a clue.

The dog plays an important role for many people. It may be a child substitute where a person can release his own deep inner emotions without fear of letting his guard down. A dog can also be the source of some need for an ego boost. It may take the form of a macho-type dog, a symbol of power whose furry is controlled by the owner, or the ego of a show dog that others will admire and be jealous of. A dog can be an instrument for the false elimination of fears; a living creature who would sacrifice its life in the duty of protecting

its owner and property. The dog is also a
great pacifier for many. When you are happy,
sad, depressed, worried, confused, etc., the
faithful dog will be there. For some it is
comforting since the dog mirrors back the
emotion. It helps many get through tough times,
while others take out their daily frustrations
on the dog. It's sad, but true.

Yes, a dog is often destined to play a
given psychological role. But what happens to
the owners when the dog doesn't play the intended role, when it doesn't provide the necessary intended ingredient? It can be a real
blow to the person's emotions. The dog is not
cooperating by not fulfilling the intended
purpose or need. The frustration is magnified.
The macho dog is a cowarding wimp, the show dog
never materializes, the child substitute runs
away, the watch dog bites the owner, and instead
of being a soothing pacifier, the dog runs wild
in the house while destroying it, causing the
owner more depression.

So what is really at the end of that
leash - a dog? Well maybe, but I believe you
will find it merely an extension, a reflection,
an object, a symbol of the owner. It possesses
the ability to fulfill or destroy a person's
most intimate emotional make-up. In other
words, a dog can make you or break you. It can
be everything or nothing. It can help or
hinder.

It is extremely important that a person
understand the true emotional implications involved in purchasing a dog. They have to be
truly honest with themselves as to why they
really want a dog. Millions of dogs yearly are
sold, given away, destroyed, disposed of and
abandoned because the owner is unable to mold
and shape the dog into the given role model.

This book and Book One are intended to help you, through proper knowledge and understanding of animal behavior, achieve your goal. Only through your understanding of the dog's mind and actions will you have a better chance of forming and molding your pet into the intended role; to fulfill your emotional needs, to communicate your message and intentions, but most importantly, to help you fully enjoy and totally appreciate this fantastic animal we call a dog.

A DOG IS OFTEN A REFLECTION AND EXTENSION OF ITS OWNER

HE IS SO GOOD WHEN WE ARE HOME —

BUT WHEN WE LEAVE!!!

2. CONCEPTS OF PROBLEM SOLVING

As a professional dog trainer I am daily exposed to all sorts of people, with many different types of problems, involving virtually every conceivable breed and age of dog. Everyone seems to think that their dog problems are unique. They rarely are. What can prove to be interesting though, is how they ended up with the problems they are now encountering.

When someone comes to me with a given problem, they are, of course, concerned with the elimination of it. They will say my dog does this or that, and then they completely and thoroughly explain the unwanted behavior. What people do not seem to understand is that whatever their problem, it is usually an extension or add-on of the true problem. To clarify what I mean, look at it this way: the problem you may now be encountering is probably the end result of some other behavioral problem that you are now, or were experiencing. To illustrate this, let's say a person says to me "I want my dog to remain in only one room but he keeps getting out." Or they say "When the dog is in the utility room it barks constantly." They tell me this is the problem. NO IT IS NOT! For me to solve this I must first ask them why the dog is locked or confined to a given room in

the first place. The answer would probably be - to
prevent the dog from relieving himself or chewing in
another room. So the true problem in this case is housebreaking. The barking, or breaking out of the given room,
is merely an extension of the real problem. Solve the
original problem, housebreaking, and the secondary problem
(barking or breaking out) is also eliminated. What most
people end up doing is compounding their problems. While
in the process of trying to solve or control one problem,
they end up creating several new ones.

Hand-shyness is another extension problem, as is
submissive wetting and aggression. These common problems
are usually caused or created by the owners. Before we
can begin to eliminate them, we again must first learn
the true problem. The above mentioned problems are all
caused in the same general manner. To illustrate this,
suppose one day, regardless of the reason, a friend or
family member made a fist, brought the fist up and punched
you right in the nose. Needless to say, you wouldn't like
that one bit. It would be even worse if you didn't have
any idea of why you were punched. You would be confused,
bewildered and upset. One thing is sure - the next time
you see an individual make a fist, you would react. You
would defend yourself, or yell or run away. You would
never forget; your mind would flash back; you would in-
stantly remember even though it only happened once, maybe even years before.

You now have a case of hand-shyness with the sight
of the fist motivating you to respond. Your dog will
react precisely as you when placed in the same type of
situation. Picture this: Your dog runs off, has an item
in its mouth, or makes some sort of a mess in the house.
So you go to the dog, bend over, reach out, point, scold,
grab the collar, or even hit him on any part of his body.
Since you are performing this ritual after the fact, the
dog cannot possibly understand why this is happening to
him. So what you end up with is a dog who will respond
to the act of bending over and reaching out; the same as
you would when faced with a person making a fist. There
is absolutely no difference. When you are faced with a
threatening gesture, you will respond. If your pet is
exposed to a threat to its survival, it too will respond.

14

If you now have a dog who reacts negatively to a person bending over and reaching out, try the following: Crouch down, get on your knees and encourage your dog to come to you – do not bend over or reach out. Also try approaching the dog by walking to him backwards; then crouch down. If your dog does not demonstrate his past negative behavior (shyness, aggression or wetting), then you will have learned your dog's behavior was merely a response to the action it was exposed to (bending over or reaching out).

It is known as cause and effect. The dog does something wrong causing you to take some sort of action against him. The end result of your actions is a dog who is aggressive, hand-shy or wets submissively – better known as the effect. One problem, many times, leads to several new, additional, unwanted problems. When we are able to track down the true problem and work properly on solving it, the other add-on problems are usually, or easily eliminated in the process.

What does all of this mean? Simply, it is rare to be able to eliminate one problem if the cause is still present. In other words, work on finding and solving the cause, not just the effect.

YOUR DOG DOESN'T HAVE A PROBLEM - YOU DO.

3. DOES HE DO IT OUT OF SPITE?

Your dog did something wrong - you know why - he did it out of spite because he is mad at you. You are sure of it. He plotted to get even. Ah, - those convenient excuses. You say he's mad because you didn't bring him with you, or he is upset because you didn't bring him to Aunt Mary's house last Saturday and she always gives him a goodie treat. Ridiculous!

As anyone will admit, a dog and a human being are not the same. So, at times, you may say, he is only a dog, he doesn't know any better. In other words, you find it convenient, at times, to place the dog into a very simple role. Yet, in virtually the very next breath, as you are trying to figure out why a certain action has taken place, you turn the dog into the most cunning of adversaries that is able to plot and plan out all kinds of things. He is an animal that lays around all day planning evil deeds in order to purposely strike back at you. I repeat, RIDICULOUS!

When a person has very little knowledge about animal behavior, he automatically reverts to looking at all situations from a human point of view. It is known as seeing things through the mind's eye. You see what you want to see. It's convenient. It answers the question. A place for everything and everything in it's place. You know you've got it all figured out; you just don't know what to do about it.

The average person does one of two things; one is reprimanding the dog after the fact (this is equivalent to spanking an older child for a bad deed), or secondly, they try to win the dog's affection back with some new treats or toys. Neither will work. You're on your way to a lot of frustration.

The simplicity of the animal mind is what most dog owners cannot seem to comprehend. Instead of being able to see the obvious, people become totally engrossed in the most complex explanations of why this or that is occurring. Not only you but your dog is in big trouble when this occurs.

If I were to ask you "Is it possible to sit and talk to a dog? Do you feel that a dog can understand the English language?" you would, of course, say "No, he is only a dog." Yet, there you are spanking or bribing the dog while saying to him "This is because of what you did hours before." You have just contradicted yourself.

Take a look at this example: Let's say you have a nine month old child and you discovered that the child relieved himself on the floor. Would you take the child to it and push his nose in it? Of course not. You could go to the child and harshly yell and scold him for doing wrong; but your actions would cause the child to start crying. Does this mean the child knows he is wrong? Again, of course not. You know the child is crying out only because of your sounds of scolding, not the words being spoken.

Your dog's mentality and ability to react is virtually the same as the child's. If each and every time the young child did wrong, you approached and then yelled, scolded, hit and dragged him, you would soon have a handshy child who would cry when approached. You know I am right. Then why is it some people do exactly these things to a dog and yet expect the dog to understand?

When looking at animal versus human communication, your best bet is to look at it this way. If you were in a foreign country where no one could speak English, what

18

would you do? You know the people don't understand what you are saying because they do not speak the same language as you. When you attempt to convey a message to a foreigner, all you will really be able to do is transmit your emotion. The foreigner would only be able to know if you are mad, happy, scared, upset, worried, confused, etc. He would not, of course, know the reasons why. The most you could hope for is a response to your actions and tones, not an answer to your question. The foreigner is in the same predicament as you are. He may be trying to answer, but alas - you don't understand a word he is saying. You are both simply having a failure to communicate.

What I want you to do is look at your dog as if it were a foreigner. Realize that he is unable to understand what you are saying. Accept the fact that what you may be seeing is only a response to your mood, tone of voice, or actions. Nothing more. He does not understand your words. A dog's actions are based on some form of survival - never on emotions. Chewing, food stealing, aggressiveness, territorial, pack instincts, den, etc. are all equated with survival by the dog.

Emotions in people come from past experiences - love, hate, resentfulness, spitefulness, etc. These emotions are developed by people. They are harbored, contemplated, acted upon, plotted, planned, carried through. This can work for you or against you. With people, a harbored thought or idea can lead to a great discovery or a disastorous evil ending.

Let's take a look at the past one thousand years. In that time man has progressed and evolved tremendously. By taking past facts and learned knowledge, man has been able to create many complex and remarkable inventions. He has turned daydreams into reality, and harbored thoughts into dreams fulfilled. The next one thousand years will bring about discoveries far beyond what we can now comprehend. But the dog, the simple dog, is today the same as it was a thousand years ago. It will continue to remain the same far into the future. The dog is incapable of harboring thoughts, of plotting or evolving any further. The one thing that they can do

very well is survive. Every action of your dog is
based on survival. As a result, it is impossible for
your dog to be spiteful. No, only you and your mind's
eye can see it that way, not your dog.

4. IT MAY LOOK LIKE CHEWING, BUT IS IT?

So you have heard and unfortunately believe, that as your dog grows older, he will grow out of certain bad habits such as chewing. You are definitely in for a surprise! Let's assume your dog has an occasional destructive and/or dangerous chewing problem. You might say that he has almost grown out of the chewing stage. I ask you now - are you sure that what you are seeing is actually chewing? Dogs appear to chew for several reasons. The average dog owner is only aware of one of the causes - teething. But there is a second and very common cause for what is happening - survival. Yes, they chew to survive. Take a look around you outside; watch the birds, squirrels, cows, horses, ants and other living things. Look closely and what do you really see? You will soon notice that all living creatures spend most of their lives seeking out food sources, constantly seeking, eating, finding and hoarding food or what may appear to be a food item.

You are no different than the other creatures around you. Look at it this way - man is the only creature with the ability to reason. We have the ability to plan our survival program rather than just live on a day to day basis as an animal does. What do you do when you get hungry? You may go out and pick up a hamburger

21

at the local drive-in or go to the refrigerator depending on your funds and/or food supply, or location. Simple, isn't it! You plan your action and then respond or react accordingly. You have hoarded food in order to survive. It is so simple. Now, I wonder what you would do if, for some reason, you found yourself lost in a jungle or on a deserted island. There are no drive-ins, your money is useless and no refrigerator stocked with food. You don't know when you are going to be rescued so you are left now with only your basic survival instincts. A need for food, water and shelter become paramount to you. Unless you were trained on survival techniques, you would begin to experiment with food sources - roots, bark, flowers, weeds, berries, etc. Besides feeling the pangs of hunger, your body would also be craving certain nutritional needs and you would try to fulfill them. One day, in your quest for food, you could end up eating the wrong thing and die. What a shame! Little did you know a rescue team was only an hour away and they had plenty of safe food available for you.

With all of this in mind, let's take a look from the dog's point of view. Remember, he does not possess the ability to reason or plan ahead as you do. He is unaware in the beginning that you will provide the feedings, the survival ingredient. Instinctively he will seek out food sources, the same as a human baby does from day one. Your goal is to teach the dog to return to a given spot to find food (his bowl). In the beginning he is totally unaware that you are going to feed him. He does not possess the ability to think - Oh boy - I eat in an hour! If he is hungry he may instinctively start to seek out food. Your dog is trapped on your own private, little island; he must make due with what is available to him. Wall paper paste smells good - he tries it; tissue paper smells sweet - he tries it; furniture polish smells nice - he tries it; the garbage, newspaper, pencils, ink, etc. all have a scent of their own. Floor wax, plastics, wood and plants all appear to be a food source. So he tries it, not to chew, but as a possible food source. You may see it as chewing - - - - but is it really???!!

In Book One I wrote about how toys, etc. can cause unintentional chewing problems; I also discussed diet.

22

If your dog is not receiving a balanced diet, his system will cry out for some missing nutrients. It is similar to when you get a craving for something sweet; you seek it out.

Your dog, in time, will learn to return to the feeding area that you have provided to find the survival food; much the same as birds return to a feeder you place in the yard. If you want to mess up this very simple and basic response, all you have to do is give your dog treats, etc. throughout the day or allow your dog to receive food in different locations. Throw his balanced diet out of wack by feeding treats, and then sit back and face the consequences. The rule of thumb is: Feed in one place only - his bowl, and stick to a balanced diet. Those pleading eyes can be hard to resist, but be sensible and your dog will soon learn to return to the food source area (his bowl) and will lose the instinct to seek out food from all of those other miscellaneous items or places.

IT MAY LOOK LIKE CHEWING –

BUT THEN AGAIN, IT JUST MIGHT NOT BE!

5. KILLING WITH KINDNESS

It is ironic but true. Many, many dogs and puppies die yearly at the hands of their devoted owners. Yes, people are the number one, indirect cause of pain, suffering and destruction of household pets. Is it done on purpose? Rarely - only a very sick mind would purposely harm an animal.

Let's take a closer look now and see if you are a potential killer through kindness. Do you ever give your dog a bone to eat? If so, it is only a matter of time before a bone harms his insides. Do you tie your dog up inside or outside and leave him unattended? Broken legs, broken jaws and strangulation could be in your dog's future. Do you feed table scraps or other means of a poor diet? Then the future physical well-being of your dog is at stake. You might as well plan on spending a lot of time and money in the future at the local vet's office. Do you beat, scold, spank, punish or reprimand your dog in the pretense of attempting to train? When you lack knowledge of the proper ways, and end up performing the above rituals, you can expect a hand-shy, bitter, run-away, obnoxious beast that you end up getting rid of. Maybe you are not guilty of the above, no not you; you love your dog. For example, you take your pet to the forest preserve every Sunday morning and let him run around to get plenty of fresh air and exercise. Aren't you kind?--NO YOU'RE NOT!! When you allow and condone running around wild and aimlessly, you may soon find that whenever your dog is outside, he will want to run, just like you taught him. Someday your dog will playfully bolt away, right under the wheels of a car. It is just a matter of time. You taught him to run, he does, and is injured. It is your fault, not the driver's.

How about this? You let your dog play with the neighbor's dog. You say he just loves to play with other dogs, so you allow it. Let's take a closer look. If your dog enjoys playing with other dogs that much, what is to prevent him from running to play with another dog that lives across the street? Those cars and trucks sure do hurt. Do you bring your pet to a friend's house to play with their dog while you visit, as many people do? You could be creating a potentially explosive situation. You know that you are just visiting and you will soon be leaving, but the dog at the friend's house doesn't know that. All of a sudden there is an intruder in your friend's dog's territory, a possible threat to his possessions. Instinctively, he may defend them or attempt to rid his turf of the intruder. Many serious dog fights start because of this act of kindness.

Out of sight - out of mind, or shall I call it the human cop-out? We are all guilty of this in one form or another but our interest right now is directed to the dog. Where I see this problem the most is with new dog owners that are using a crate. The proper use of a crate, especially with the young pup, is the number one, most important, paramount thing a person can do. (All of this was fully covered in Book One.)

Unfortunately, though, a very large segment of people think with their hearts instead

of their heads. Here is what I mean - I hear
this over and over: People will say "Yes we
have a crate and use it." Fine. When and how
do they use it? They will reply "When we leave
the house and that is it." What they are really
saying to me is: We love the crate; with it we
know that when we come home there will be no
messes in the house to clean up and nothing will
be chewed. They are so very happy about that.

What they are really doing is thinking
only of themselves. When they can't see the dog
in the crate (out of sight - out of mind) they
are able to accept it. But, ask the people to
crate the dog periodically throughout the day,
or night, well--- that is another thing entirely.
Example: The owner may say that when the children are playing on the floor with their toys,
the dog is a pest; or when company visits, the
dog is a pest. If I were to ask just exactly
what it is they want their dog to do at these
times, they would say to just behave, lay there,
etc. Well, by gosh, teach that dog what to do,
but not by scolding, hitting, or other obnoxious
actions; crate the dog in the children's play
area; expose him to these situations; teach him
how to behave. Use the crate to your advantage.

I pointed out in Book One about how ironic
it is to hear people say that their dog has a
chewing problem, but yet they feel that putting
the dog in a crate, when they are not home, is
cruel. To me, the chewing is dangerous and can
injure or even kill the dog. The people, in
their attempt to be kind by not wanting to crate
their dog, run the risk of injuring or killing
their pet by giving it the opportunity to chew.
The point here is - never forget that you are
dealing with an animal, a creature that sees
the world in a totally different way than you do.
It is not a wrong way - just different. Thus -
I call these situations "Killing with Kindness"!

ARE THEY REALLY PLAYING,

OR POSSESSING?

6. TESTING - HOW TO ELIMINATE THE CRATE

If you have followed the advice I gave in Book One, to use a crate for housebreaking, you are probably wondering just when you can let the dog have the freedom of the home. I hear that question often. There is no sure answer. Some dogs are ready at six months while others won't be ready until they are about a year old. Some people are overly anxious to let the dog out. They slowly become lax in the training only to find out the hard way that the pup wasn't ready for freedom yet.

By now you should notice that the dog is reasonably good while you are at home and it's true that the dog may be just as good while you are gone. But finding out can prove to be dangerous and sometimes costly. That is, unless you do it properly. Here is how I recommend you test your dog's behavior while you are gone. I could suggest that you install TV monitors all over your house, but that just isn't practical. So instead, try to find a way to block off one complete room; it doesn't matter which room. Now for the test. Place the crate in that room and put the dog in it but do not close the crate door. In almost all cases, the first half hour is the most risky; so that should be your limit in the first test. In order to find out what your dog has been doing while you are gone calls for a little preplanning. Here are some ideas: Leave a dish towel hanging somewhere with a mousetrap taped to the back side. Place a sock on the floor with a mousetrap under it. Put a mousetrap

BOOBY TRAP AN AREA

on the window ledge. Leave a magazine or newspaper on
the end table with a mousetrap under the first page. In
other words, booby-trap the entire room. By doing so
several things will be accomplished. When you come back
a half hour later, you can check the traps. If they have
not been set off, then it is reasonably safe to assume
that the dog was behaving itself while you were gone.
But, if you come home and find some mousetraps set off,
you will then know that the dog is not yet ready for
freedom. An additional plus to using this method is
that if the dog did set off some mousetraps, it more
than likely received a surprise correction from them.
Your dog is not ready for total freedom until you can
leave for at least one hour (preferably two hours) and
find everything intact as you left it. I caution you —
do not try testing without at least a few booby trapped
items. It only takes a couple of minutes to set it up
and it could mean the difference between life and death
to your dog. Also, be sure to leave the crate available
and the door open. If things go as they should, the
crate will have taught your dog by now to lay around and
sleep while you are not around and it will want to be in
his bed (the crate) during your absence.

Most people by now will have noticed that the dog
loves his crate. If you have raised him properly, this
should be the case. After testing and finding out that
your dog is behaving when left alone, you can eliminate
the crate. But if you have space, it would be nice to
keep the crate as a bed for the dog, leaving the door
open for him. You can also add a rug or something
similar at this time for the added comfort if you like,
providing the dog does not chew it.

LEAVE THE CRATE OPEN AND ACCESSIBLE –

REMEMBER IT'S HIS BED.

7. IS YOUR DOG TOO OLD TO LEARN ?

A frequently asked and yet very misunderstood question concerns the older dog. People consistently ask if their dog is too old to be trained. The unique part is that this question is asked by people who own dogs in every age group. Some feel their dog is too old to learn at one year, while others feel that at one year the dog is still too young to start training. The truth of the matter is that your dog is never too young or too old to learn. It has been said that a dog reaches its full mental capacity at four months of age and that man reaches his full capacity at around age eighteen. I don't really know how much truth there is to those statements, but let us assume they are correct. Let's take a look at man's situation first.

Suppose a man or woman is forty years old and has been doing the same job or has been in the same occupation for the past twenty years. That person is very set in his ways. Can he change his lifestyle? Can he learn a new occupation? Of course he can. Let's say he went to a trade school to learn a new occupation, then after several months of study, he would have learned a new trade. He would not have increased his intelligence; he simply would have added to his knowledge of a given situation or subject. In time, this new knowledge and new occupation would replace the old lifestyle. Man is never too old to learn to change and neither is a dog. Remember that a dog has a brain. The only problem is in the understanding of how it functions.

It has also been said that the brain is the most neglect-
ed organ, meaning we use only a slight percentage of its
true ability. Man and dog are guilty of the same thing.
We use only enough of the brain's potential as is deemed
necessary to survive. Survival is the strongest instinct
that any human or animal possesses. Just observe the
creatures around you - watch the birds, squirrels, even
the lowly fly. Watch them in their quest to survive.
Watch the fly move when you attempt to swat it. Watch
the creatures find food and run from danger signals.
Every living thing acts upon survival. For example, if
you found yourself in what you considered a life and
death situation, your mind would take over; nothing else
would matter at the moment. You would attempt to find a
way to survive. After doing so, you would have learned
something. You would have learned to never allow yourself to get into that situation again. You would not
have become more intelligent, only more knowledgeable.

Survival - it is seen by what is known as "the
mind's eye". Regardless of your age, if you were robbed
at a given spot at a certain time, you would have learned
to never expose yourself to that same situation again.
You would not want it to happen again. Survival!! Your
older dog is no different. He is set in his ways, but
they can be changed. We can use the survival instincts
to do so. I am not advocating or recommending physical
or mental harm or threats to be used on a dog. I am
merely trying to point out to you how a dog's mind
functions.

The only difference between training a young dog as
opposed to an older dog is mathematics. The young dog,
who committed an evil deed only a few times, is much
easier to modify than the older dog who committed the
same evil deed hundreds of times. Any type of training
is based on repetition, which means performing a given
act over and over again until it becomes automatic. Your
dog can get very proficient at performing a bad deed just
as easily as a good deed if you allow it - or cause it to
occur on a day to day basis. Your dog can be changed or
modified in the same manner. It is just that it will take
a little longer with the older dog. To illustrate this,
here is another example of what I mean; Suppose I were

34

to grab you and push you into a closet and immediately shut the door. Your very first reaction would be to get out. Your mind would be working on that goal. Suppose I then opened the door after thirty seconds and let you out and in the process I gave you a thousand dollars. After repeating this a few times, and giving you the thousand dollars each time, you would soon be walking into the closet on your own! A situation that, at first, was threatening to your survival is now something to look forward to. There is no danger, only rewards, but you didn't know that in the beginning.

Now, here is the same situation with a dog. Suppose you have a two-year old dog that relieves himself in the house. This dog is going to have to learn to be in a crate or dog cage. The understanding and proper use of a crate is extremely important. (See Book One for more information on dog crates.) Try this - Bring the dog to the open crate and attempt to put him into it. If he has never been in a crate before, he may put up an awful fuss and refuse to go into it. (Just like you did with the closet.) When you finally are successful in getting him in, the dog's first reaction is to get out, the same as you would. Now, let the dog out after about thirty seconds and immediately put him back in. Give him happy talk and praise while he is in; sound excited and be exuberant. Do not use a pathetic tone of voice that says - don't be scared, don't worry. The dog needs that thousand dollars - give it to him in the form of happy exuberance in your voice and attitude. (When he is out of the crate, slightly ignore him.) After about five times in and out of the crate, your dog will begin to relax while inside the crate. Lay down along side of the crate and talk to him. Make it very pleasant. Slowly begin to increase the amount of time he is in the crate - five minutes, then out, fifteen minutes, then out, etc. As you get to the longer intervals, you can give him a treat such as a ball or Nylabone to occupy him. In just one day of in and out of the crate training, your dog will have learned to accept his new environment. After two or three days, he will look forward to it. He is not more intelligent, only more knowledgeable. He is never too old to learn!

HE IS NEVER TOO OLD TO LEARN

8. AGGRESSIVE OR AN OBNOXIOUS ATTITUDE FORMING

An often-heard complaint is that of a person having a normal dog that seems to be getting more and more aggressive day after day. They say that he gets vicious acting or sounding when someone walks by the house or comes to the door. They say that at all other times he is so good and has never bitten anyone, but he seems, at times, to be turning mean. They also say "We have never hit him or had any trouble; what is going wrong?" As the saying goes - "You can't see the forest for the trees." (This is merely another case of Cause and Effect.)

My first question might be - do you have a fenced-in yard? If not, do you tie the dog up outside? Odds are the people do one or the other. Here is what can be taking place from the dog's point of view. This is one of those situations where the kind act of fencing in your yard in order to give the dog fresh air and exercise can work against you. As with everything else, let's look at this example in a forward step-by-step sequence. Let's assume the dog is in a fenced yard (the cause). The dog is very happy and content on his own little island. Instinctively, he will protect his territory from intruders. So it begins; you let the dog out into the yard and he is just loping around. Then someone walks past the house. At the first startling sight of someone, your dog gives out a little woof. And, lo and behold, the intruder continues on, away from the territory. As far as your dog is concerned, he just scared the intruder away.

Slowly the pattern forms - someone walks by, your dog barks, the person continues on.

Each day the mailman walks toward the house. Your dog barks, but the mailman continues to approach. He barks again and again and, finally, the dog notices the intruder is now leaving. Your dog is now beginning to build up his ego (the effect). You have the start of a Macho dog on your hands. As far as the dog is concerned, all of these strangers that approach or pass by are a threat to his survival, his territory and possessions (you) must be protected. He barks (they leave) and (he) continues to bark until they leave. Keep in mind that when you allow something to take place, you are condoning it; acutally, you are training the dog. This situation can get out of hand if you do not "nip it in the bud". Certainly a woof or two is alright as long as you still have control of the situation and are able to quiet the dog on command. If you see this problem forming or have it already, this is what I suggest. As with so many of the other things that we have discussed, you must re-create the problem. You have got to know when the dog is going to act up. Try this: Arrange for someone to walk by or come to the door at a specific time; let's say 5:00 p.m. You, knowing what is about to happen, must be prepared to take control. Several minutes before 5:00 p.m. position yourself so that you can take control of the dog as soon as he begins to act up. Outdoors or indoors, a throw can or jug should do the trick. (A reminder: A throw can is a soda can with six pennies in it or a plastic milk jug can be used with a handful of small rocks inside for the purpose of noise.)

After the dog has barked once or twice at the pre-arranged intruder, command the dog to shut-up - to be quiet - and throw the noise item at or near him. It should shut him up. Have an extra throw item handy just in case it is needed. As soon as the dog quiets down, go to him and praise. He did his job. He alerted you and then obeyed your orders to be quiet. I'm sure you are wondering how this will affect your dog as a watch dog. Your dog will learn that when you are around you are in charge and when you are gone, he takes over.

(For more information on the forming of aggressive behavior, read Chapter Nine - The Spoiled Dog.)

(In Chapter Fifteen you will find a reprint of an article and experiment I conducted concerning dogs and burglars. I believe you will find it shockingly interesting.)

AGGRESSIVE BEHAVIOR CAN START TO FORM

FROM SOMETHING AS INNOCENT AS A FENCED—IN YARD

9. THE SPOILED DOG

This will probably be one of the most curiously read chapters, because who hasn't spoiled their dog in some form or another? You know it - you admit it - now, let's face it! The ways in which to spoil a dog run the gamut from A to Z. Let's take a look at some of the ramifications and consequences of letting it get out of control. Spoiling a dog usually ends up creating a bad nuisance or frustrating habit by the dog. At the other end of the scale is the dog who has become so spoiled that it is down-right dangerous to have around.

Spoiling the dog begins innocently enough. Here are a few simple examples - the dog, as a pup, may whine and you go to it and pet it or let it outside. You may feel at this time - Oh good, he's letting me know when he wants to go out. Now, as an older dog, he whines or barks constantly; oh, it starts so innocently. Maybe one day your dog or pup doesn't eat properly, so you worry and entice him to eat by giving something you consider more appetizing. The end result is a fussy eater that you are constantly catering to and feeding improperly.

Maybe it is a deep psychological problem within all of us. Could it be that you, yourself, desire to be treated in a catering manner, to be waited upon, worried about, soothed, comforted, protected and cared for? Do you transmit your own personal inner desires through your pet? Probably.

41

As I mentioned earlier, kindness (spoiling) applied improperly can cause harm to your pet. Throughout this book I have been pointing out many of the different ways in which your acts of kindness can be misinterpreted by your pet and cause more harm than good. Yes, the spoiled dog can be a real nuisance to have around. What I'm concerned about now though, is the dog that becomes dangerous as a result of your (kind) actions.

Hopefully, I can clearly present to you how this can occur. First, here is a little background. A dog, being a pack animal, instinctively will follow the leader. To the young pup, mom is boss. As the pup grows older, somewhere between four months to one year, an instinctive response takes place. It is time for the young dog to find out if it is a leader of the pack or merely part of the pack. Keep in mind, that when the pup does not have other dogs or animals around, you and your family become the pack. It usually starts innocently looking enough; the very young pup claims an area or an item and growls or barks when you approach him. He is so small and young that it looks cute; so you laugh it off - you pass it off as only playing. (A point of interest is that a dog is rarely playing; they are practicing, trying out, or rehearsing instinctive responses they were born with, most based on survival.) Things become dangerous when your dog starts to develop a leadership role. If, through your actions, you have allowed your dog to be-lieve that he is the leader of the pack, you, your family and friends, can be in very serious trouble.

The overly spoiled dog will play one of two parts; confused is one of them. This type of dog doesn't know its role in life. It lacks confidence, is fearful, and doesn't recognize the pack leader. That, of course, is supposed to be you. The confusion that creates fear forces the dog to take aggressive and protective action in any situation that looks like a threat to its own survival. Small dog or large, those canine teeth can sure cause pain and injury, unpleasant - but true.

The other role a spoiled dog may take is that of pack leader. As it was growing up, it may have virtually done anything (and everything) it wanted to do. The instinctive role of your newly created pack leader is simple. He will protect the pack from all outside dangers; he will keep his pack in line by demonstrating his number one position and he will do virtually anything he wants. In other words, your dog becomes an obnoxious beast. He runs through the house, knocks everything down, steals items, harrasses the neighbors, nips at your hands; he is totally out of control. Anything can happen at this point.

You have probably heard the phrase - Ruling the Roost or the Pecking Order. We use them as expressions when making a statement. But, do you know where these sayings came from or what they really mean? A test was conducted many years ago with chickens. Some very interesting observations resulted. I'll omit the technical aspects and simply relate the basic findings of the test. This is essentially what occurred - twelve chickens were placed in a pen. For days they lived and ate together out of a single tub of food. It was observed that, even though the chickens ate together, they approached the food tub one at a time. The chickens were then numbered and it was found that the same one approached the food first daily, followed by number two, then three, etc. It was noted that each chicken knew its rightful place. They call this the Pecking Order. They wondered what would happen if an additional chicken was added to the pack; so an outsider was admitted. Throughout the day confrontations occured; something was happening. When feeding time arrived, it was noted that the new chicken approached the food tub in the number seven position and from then on continued to apporach as number seven. What this means is that the new chicken found it could basically defeat six of the chickens but not the other six. His place in its society became number seven. Thus the sayings - Pecking Order, Ruling the Roost, or Chain of Command.

Your dog is no different. When you obtain a pet and bring it into your home, it is immediately confronted with your family's chain of command. It must learn to be in the proper place in your household or pack. It must realize that you rule the roost, that the chain of command begins with you and works down. All of the members of

43

your family must hold a position above the dog. This
certainly is not accomplished by beating the dog. It is
accomplished by simple understanding of the animal mind,
and taking a firm stand, while asserting your authority.
One of the ways of doing this is through obedience training. It is an opportunity to properly assert your authority. What I mean is if you say stay, by gosh, you mean
it; or come, or sit, and then properly following through
to implant the message - I am the boss and this is how
it is going to be done. I repeat, harshness or brutality
is unnecessary, just a firm mental attitude on your part.
Wherever you live, there are obedience schools and clubs;
some good, some bad. Look into them, observe what is
going on, ask questions. If you like what you see, sign
up. You'll be glad you did. Think of it this way - if
a chicken can do it, so can you!

RULING THE ROOST

10. SHY DOG -
OR IS HE AFRAID ?

One of the most common mistakes of dog owners is in what I call "reading your dog". Simply, it means, seeing your dog do something and properly understanding what is meant by his actions. Probably, the two most misunderstood reactions concern times when you are sure that the dog knows he is wrong (he doesn't) and secondly, when you feel the dog is afraid or shy.

Let's take a closer look at the shy dog syndrome. Suppose you have a timid dog and you are at the veterinarian's office. You and the dog are sitting there waiting your turn. You notice that the dog is shaking and appearing very worried about these new surroundings. You look around and see nothing frightening, so you reach down or pick up the dog and start petting him. In a very reassuring voice you begin telling him that it's okay, don't worry, everything is fine. Your dog continues to shake, so you continue to sooth. WRONG!! This is such an easy mistake to make, but potentially harmful. In reality, what you are doing is praising the dog for his actions. Keep in mind that the dog cannot understand the words that you are saying, only the tone in which he hears them. That tone is more of an encouraging and praising one in it's delivery. You sit there, virtually saying to the dog with your nice, calm tone - good boy, that's the way, shake, that's what you should do, keep it up, I'm proud of you, yea! You are now well on your way to teaching your dog how to act fearful in strange situations.

ARE YOU CAUSING OR CURING FEAR?

And so it continues, time after time; you take your dog somewhere new, he shakes, you praise. Wow, what a mistake! The ramifications of this innocent act of praising shyness <u>can lead to a very insecure dog</u>.

As discussed in Chapter Three, suppose someone came up to you and started talking to you in a foreign language. You didn't know what was being said, so you would simply react to the tone you were hearing. The tone would give you some indication of that foreigner's intentions. Is the stranger angry at you, happy to see you and so on? You pick up on the tone and act accordingly. I suppose you could go to a foreign language dictionary and look up the meanings of the sounds you are hearing, but your dog is unable to do that. As a result, all the dog is able to do is respond to the sounds. By encouraging the dog to be timid, you will have successfully trained him to be just that; a timid, shy, frightened dog (a classic failure to communicate).

An insecure dog is one who is in, what I call, the middle of the road. What I mean is, he doesn't know right from wrong. He is somewhere in between the two. Have you ever had a fear, heard a strange sound, been in an unfamiliar situation such as a new job? You are insecure; you are worried and confused. The fears go away as soon as you feel comfortable about your surroundings. As soon as you learn that the sounds you hear are not a threat to your well being, you give a sigh of relief. As soon as you learn about the new job, you feel comfortable about where you are. Your dog is no different. Soothing, praising and avoiding situations can only <u>compound his insecurities</u> (as discussed in Chapter Two). The answer is simple. As with any other kind of problem with your dog, in order to work it out of him, you must recreate the scene. This may prove to be time consuming, but definitely worthwhile. Make a list of environments that you know are traumatic to your dog when he is exposed to them. Now, starting with the simplest and least traumatic, recreate it or go to it. If he is scared of the vacuum cleaner, put the dog on leash, sit down in a comfortable chair a few feet away and turn the vacuum cleaner on. In time, maybe even hours, the dog will calm down; then start your praise. In other words, <u>praise the</u>

47

positive, not the negative. He must learn it is only noise and will not hurt him. Repeat as often as necessary until you have accomplished your goal.

Let's assume your dog is worried about the vet's waiting room. Simply go to the vet and ask permission to sit in the waiting room for a couple of hours for several days. Bring along a good book and sit there. Put your foot on the leash and ignore the dog. Try not to let him push up against your leg or hide under the chair. In time he will calm down. Then start to praise. Repeat as many times as is necessary until the dog is behaving as you want him to. After you have concluded one situation, move onto the next. Sure, it is time consuming, but if you care about your pet, you will find the time to expose him to these situations and build up his confidence.

There is an irony to this type of advice. It concerns the dog owner's misunderstanding of the term - dog training. When the average dog owner refers, or thinks about training, he narrows it down to physical. He virtually defines dog training as heel, sit, stay, etc. This sort of person will spend many, many hours practicing these exercises. Of course this is fine, but what must be clearly understood is that dog training is much more far ranging. Training a dog to not be afraid of a vacuum cleaner or vet's office is just as important, if not more important, than teaching the dog to lay down on command.

Training means behavior modification. When applied properly, the owner and the dog both reap the benefits. Yes, training comes in many forms. The way the shy dog is encouraged to continue to be shy as well as the advice on how to combat the problem is but one example. You are teaching, and your dog is learning something each and every day. Be very aware of this and you will find that the source of your problem as well as the cure, has been right in front of you all of the time. Open your eyes and see if you are being the cause or the cure. Try learning how to "read your dog" (or thinking of it from your dog's point of view).

In essence, he must learn that noise does not hurt, sounds do not hurt, and people do not hurt.

11. APARTMENT AND CONDO RESIDENTS

This chapter is directed to apartment and condo residents, but the information contained will be of interest to all dog owners. These situations are so common, I felt they should be included in this book.

PROBLEM ONE

Not many condo or apartment residents are able to install a dog run in the yard. Therefore, they are forced to walk the dog on leash. As a result, this becomes a frequent occurrence: People say "I take the dog out and walk him regularly, sometimes for a half of an hour or more, but the dog does not relieve himself." Then, when they return home, they take the leash off and turn the dog loose. Within a very short time, the dog relieves itself in the home, usually in another room, out of sight. The owner surely becomes frustrated with this one, and yet the solution is ridiculously simple.

Two things must be done for absolute results. First, let's take a look at why it happens. In every case, the dog owner is using too short of a leash. The dog, being held in check, is put into a situation quite similar to a dog placed in a crate. The dog will often not relieve itself when contained to a small area, in this case, the radius of the leash. Simply walk the dog on a long rope instead of the leash. A twelve to fifteen foot long rope would be fine. In other words, give the dog more area

51

and the opportunity to get a greater distance away from you. It is possible that you may have already taught the dog not to relieve itself while on any kind of leash. If the dog still does not relieve itself when walked on the rope, then as soon as you get home, crate the dog. Repeat your walk a little later. The law of nature says that sooner or later the dog will have to relieve itself. Within one day your dog should get the idea, but continue this for at least a week or more. In other words, if the dog does not relieve itself when walked, do not give him freedom of the home; when you return, crate him instead. Freedom in the home is to be allowed only when you feel it is safe to do so. Consistency on your part will lead to consistency and reliability on the dog's part.

PROBLEM TWO

Apartment and condo dwellers have a unique problem of their own not faced by home owners. In a multiple housing unit there can be numerous outside noises. People are coming and going from work at different hours of the day or night; guests of neighbors visiting at different times; children going in and out, etc. As a result, an established pattern of noise and sound is impossible. It also becomes impossible for the dog to pick out a strange sound in the night. If the dog barks at all sounds, the neighbors will soon be angry at you and justifiably so. Your dog does not have the ability to distinguish all sounds. He cannot reason - that sounds like a good guy and that sounds like a bad guy. The environment usually does not have a repetitious enough pattern for the dog to pick-up on, and if you think about it, you will find that you are also unable to sort out all the sounds. The facts are, if you live in an apartment or condo, your chances of having a watch dog are virtually nil. Only a quiet dog is suitable for this type of environment. Do not let the bad habit of barking begin. If your older dog is already a barker when you are gone, the only thing you can do is change his habit by changing his lifestyle and environment. It is simple enough. Get a crate and teach the dog that it must be quiet while inside of it. Use the noise cans or jugs as mentioned before to accomplish this quiet behavior. Do this: Place the dog in the crate and recreate a sound

such as noise in the hallway. If the dog begins barking,
charge into the room and throw a noise item at the crate.
It cannot hurt the dog; it will only teach him that the
act of barking causes a very unpleasant reaction to occur.
He will soon learn to be quiet in the crate. Leave the
dog in the crate whenever you go out. Your neighbors
will thank you for your efforts. Try it - it works.

A GOOD DOG IS WELCOME ANYWHERE

12. WHAT IS A COLLAR ?

The dog collar is a very misunderstood item. They come in a variety of types. I could probably write a whole book on just this one subject, but let's stick to the basics. Collars run from cutsie rhinestone to electronic and everything in-between. The two most common collars are the plain buckle collar and the slip collar. A slip collar is often improperly called a choke collar. As a result, many people use a buckle collar assuming it doesn't choke, nonsense. A buckle collar used on a dog that pulls on a leash causes pressure on the front of the dog's neck and will choke. Many times a dog that is walked regularly or tied up outside with a buckle collar on, will cough excessively due to injury to the front of its neck. It can have the same effect as punching your dog in the vital neck area. A slip collar, used on the same dog, utilizes all of the muscles around the dog's neck and actually takes pressure off of the front area. In other words, the pressure is uniform around the dog's neck rather than centralized to one frontal spot. Secondly, a dog can slip out of a buckle collar but not from a <u>properly fitted slip collar</u>. So, yes, I am recommending a slip collar. A slip collar is a relatively inexpensive item but it is amazing to see how many people buy extra large ones because the dog is going to grow into it - false and foolish economy. A properly fitted slip collar should have no more than two inches of play when snug around the dog's neck. You should be prepared to buy several during the growing time of the larger breeds.

Slip collars come in three different materials — leather, nylon and chain. When your dog is younger and growing, use the nylon. When he gets older you can use any type. If you use the chain type, keep away from any that have large links of chain. It should slide smoothly through the rings. Big links tend to hang up. I also suggest that no collar be left on your dog when at home. Gruesome stories of strangulation are much too common among dogs who were unnecessarily wearing their collars.

Other points about a collar are, if you own more than one dog, then you have noticed that when they play they grab each other by the neck. If you were to leave collars on the dogs, one of them could easily get its jaw caught on the other's collar while playing — very dangerous. In most areas, tags attached to a dog's collar is the law. Most people place an I.D. tag and rabies tag together. As most of you know, a dog's hearing is better than ours. Do you realize that those tags, jangling on the dog's collar, can prove to be very unpleasant to the dog? Everyone seems to do this and I'll never understand why. In order to eliminate the noise the tags can cause, all you have to do is disperse them around the dog's collar just like a charm bracelet. It is a little more pleasant for your pet.

13. WHAT IS A LEASH ?

A leash, according to Webster, is a cord, strap, etc. by which a <u>dog</u> or the like is <u>held</u> in check.

Well, it seems that Webster knows very little about training - for if he did, he would realize that a LEASH is a correction device attached to a dog's collar for the purpose of helping to teach a dog the difference between right and wrong. It is to be used as needed and should <u>never</u> be used as merely a restraint. A leash is so abused and misused as well as being totally misunderstood. It's time dog owners knew the purpose of this item if they expect the dog to understand the intended messages it will transmit.

Here is but one of many typical mistakes made by new dog owners. You purchase an eight week old pup, then run to the local pet shop to purchase a leash and collar. This is what unfortunately can happen. You place the leash and collar on the dog and attempt to walk only to find that the pup fights this new contraption. It puts on the brakes, it cries out, it wants to go in every direction except the one you want it to go. So what do you do - you start sweet talking the pup. You say very nicely, "Come on, let's go, it's okay" etc. You are trying to sooth and relax the pup. Well, you did it again; you goofed. You know very well what you are saying and attempting to explain to your pup, but the dog, not being able to understand your words, can only relate to the tones in which it hears. Those tones from you are happy and encouraging. They come across as praise to the dog. Yes, you are praising the dog's negative behavior. You are inadvertently encouraging this type of behavior when on a leash and collar, while at the same time, teaching the pup not to come in your direction, but instead, to go the other way. Now your mind says to you - gee it looks like my pup wants to run away; I had better continue to keep him on this leash. So it begins, a daily training session of poor behavior on the leash.

This need not happen. A pup, as mentioned many times, is a pack animal and will instinctively follow. The leash and collar placed on too young a dog, is a threat to survival; it is scarey. You would be much better off to do all of the same encouraging minus the leash. You will find the pup will follow. The leash is unnecessary. Now, of course, a little common sense should be applied here. If you live next to a highway or have an older dog, this shouldn't be tried. What I recommend then is a long line instead of a short leash. A fifteen foot piece of rope with a bolt snap on the end will work much better. Try this: Attach the dog to the long line (15 feet) and let him wander. Now give a little snap action. Yes, your dog will still panic a bit, but keep doing it. Just keep on tugging on your end of the rope. Do not pull. Here is what will happen: Your dog, being fifteen feet away from you, will soon realize that it is a frightening world away from you and that it had better return back to you. When it begins to come in your direction start your praise and happy talk. Because of the greater distance away from you (15 feet) you will have time to praise the positive response, that of coming to you. A short leash only allows you time to praise the negative response. Simple, isn't it!

A point of interest - I have found in talking to thousands of people that for everyone who ties their dog up outside for fresh air and exercise, nine out of ten people report that, given the opportunity, their dog would run away if turned loose. I have several ideas on why this occurs, but more important, is the advice. I never recommend tieing a dog out. Instead I recommend a pen in your yard as mentioned and described in Book One.

Penned up dogs are no where near as likely to run off as a tied up dog will.

When it does come time for a proper leash, I suggest a six foot nylon or leather one. A chain leash is so impractical. I guess people think it is stronger; it isn't! Also, if your dog pulls on the leash, a chain can sure hurt your own hands. That's not all; think about all of that extra weight attached to the dog's neck. A true statement is that a chain is only as strong as its weakest link. Even with a nylon or leather leash, a piece of metal will be used as a bolt snap. Take a look at the bolt and how the snap is attached to the material. Many times you will find a very weak link at that point.

DOES THE LEASH AND COLLAR YOU ARE NOW USING MAKE SENSE?

14. CASES FROM MY FILES

My records, charts, graphs and recollections of problems that I have heard could fill many volumes. I have found that a great number of people are embarrassed or ashamed of the dog problems they are experiencing. They will be very candid with me and yet minimize their problems to friends, neighbors and relatives. This is really very understandable. For who wants to admit that they are failing in the raising of their pet. Who wants to brag about how well their dog lifts its leg on the furniture? No one wants to exclaim the joys of a dog who is terrorizing the family. Who wants to declare – my dog is driving me crazy? Well, remember this – the same as you may minimize the problems you are having, odds are good that your friends are also doing the same with you.

Presented here is simply a minute sampling of the problems I hear day after day. They represent only a part of the eighty-eight separate problem categories, and yet even though each person's problem is slightly different, at the same time they are all very similar. The differences only occur because of the household in which they originate. In some cases, the dog may come from a household in which the youngest resident is over seventy, while the next dog may be a product of a household of much younger people with several youngsters as part of the environment. No two households are exactly alike, so no two dogs or dog problems, will be exactly alike. This is why it is so important that the human elements involved become better educated in the understanding of animal behavior.

The following problems are merely a sample. It should make you feel better knowing you are not alone.

The first case is of the person who tied his dog to a water pipe in the upstairs bathroom, then left for the day. When he returned, he found the dog had chewed through the wall and broke the water pipe causing a virtual flood downstairs.

Then we have the lady who invited her friends over for coffee and cake. After seating them, the family pet jumped up on the table, snarled and proceeded to eat everyone's cake. All of the ladies were too scared to stop him.

A household of elderly people related the frustration of attempting to catch their dog, who was running wildly throughout the house, carrying a Norman Rockwell gift in his mouth.

Another lady said "Everytime I sit down to watch television, the dog walks up to it and lifts his leg on it." She said that is bad enough, but if she attempts to sit on the floor, the dog tries to wet on her.

Then we have the minister and family who related their pet won't let anyone into their home. He said "In my position, this just cannot be allowed."

On and on it goes. Here are a few others received in their own words.

BREED OF DOG - GERMAN SHEPHERD

Shows aggressive behavior when being corrected
(Bares teeth)
Chews - wallpaper, people

BREED OF DOG - TERRIER

Continues to urinate in the house even though
    he is taken out frequently
Aggressive behavior - strains at leash wanting to
    run to strangers. Acts vicious and I do be-
    lieve he'd bite. Has in the past turned on
    owners.
Growls and barks when scolded for biting owner's
    shoes, then runs about in a frenzy.
Stubborn when given commands.

BREED OF DOG - POODLE

Steals shoes and toys and hides under table.
Doesn't chew, but growls and bares teeth if
    cornered with a stolen item.
Needs to be taught to come on command.
Barks while outside (continually).

BREED OF DOG - LABRADOR RETRIEVER

Daily problem - charging and barking at neighbors
    in their yard or people passing by on the road.
Daily - garbage stealing from kitchen waste
    basket.
Daily - stool eating (AGGA!)
Occasional problem - growling/barking at visitors
    in our home even though: a) they have visited
    before and have been kind to her, b) a newcomer
    gets up after being in house 2-3 hours and she
    barks/growls and makes an effort to charge at
    them. She has not bitten anyone yet, but we
    are fearful of this.

BREED OF DOG - DOBERMAN

Cowers when disciplined.

BREED OF DOG - MIX

Biting of myself and daughter, age 5. (For some
    reason this is at its worst in the morning.)
Jumping up on ourselves, others, furniture, walls,

etc.   Pulling things down.
Teasing (grabbing something and running off with
    it, chewing on things when we aren't looking
    or aren't in the room, going into "forbidden"
    area of house when we aren't watching).
Not coming to us when called (outside especially).
Digging outside.
Barking (unnecessary kind).

BREED OF DOG - COCKER SPANIEL

Does not take correction. Defies us and repeats
    same act, no matter how forceful the correction
    or the type of correction (very persistent).
Nipping at our wrists or sleeve and pant cuffs.
    Nips at us when we correct him.
Growls or barks at us when we correct him.

BREED OF DOG - COLLIE

Dog wetting when guests come. Dog does not know
    he's wetting. He seems so excited and happy
    to see people that if they bend over to pet
    him, he wets.
Basic housebreaking.

BREED OF DOG - GOLDEN RETRIEVER

1. Two weeks ago she chewed top right side off of
    living room chair.
2. When my daughter's friends come in, she always
    jumps on them. We have to hold her all the
    time now.
3. Goes crazy when she sees another dog outside.
4. Constantly jumps up with front paws on counter
    in kitchen, also on the table when we are
    eating.
5. Garbage is put out of her way (and ours, too)
    cause she is too nosy.
6. When kids or other dogs go by (she can see them
    out of front window) she barks constantly.
7. Last summer we used to play catch until the time
    she ran away from me and I had a hard time
    getting her back.

As mentioned at the beginning of this book, you and your family play an important part in the raising and behavior of your pet. Your dog will become a product and symbol of your actions and knowledge. YOU WILL ULTIMATELY BE THE CAUSE AND/OR THE CURE!

15. WHAT'S IT
ALL ABOUT ?

The story you are about to read is true. I wrote it the following morning, after it happened, while all of the facts were still very clear to me. After writing it, I submitted it to two of the leading dog publications, Off Lead and Front & Finish. After they printed the story, I received many responses and reactions from people throughout the United States and two other countries. Other news publications and writers, such as Lissa Kaplan of the Dayton Daily News, Ohio, asked permission to use, reprint and/or write on the subject. I knew a story of this nature would cause conjecture and controversy. But, as I said, it is true, it did happen.

You are invited to form your own conclusions. After you have read this, you will know why I titled it

"WHAT'S IT ALL ABOUT?"

This past week I had the opportunity to conduct a very unique experiment. It all started with a phone call I received from a police detective assigned to one of the large metropolitan towns in my area. He told me they were having a very difficult time solving a rash of robberies in their town. When I asked just how I could help, he related this story to me.

The detective told me the problem started about five months ago and that someone was breaking into homes while the people were asleep. In the process of tabulating evidence and clues, they try to come up with a profile of the burglar. When there are many robberies taking place, many times one per night, a pattern starts to form. The robberies always took place between 2:00 a.m. and 5:00 a.m. In this case, they noticed not only the pattern of what time it would take place, but also by using a map with pins to identify the addresses, it became clear in what part of town the burglary would occur.

Many other facts started to emerge in the course of their investigations. One of the facts which became obvious was that at least 85 percent of the homes burglarized had one or more dogs and yet, not once did the victims report being awoken by their dog's barking. It seemed strange to the detective that these dogs didn't sound off. He noticed when he was conducting his investigations at the victims' homes that all of the dogs barked. Some started barking as a result of seeing him, while others barked at merely the noise of him approaching the house. He also noted that the reports of the other officers and technicians involved in the case made mention of an aggressive dog on the premises and that many homeowners were reported as being surprised their dog did not alert them of the intruder. In many of the cases, the burglar was bold enough to break a window to get in. Yet, even with all of that noise, not once did the people or dogs wake up. Why?

His question was intriguing. It was obvious that you could not immobilize a dog with a gas spray or other similar device because the burglar would have to enter the home first to do so and no dog barked at the sound of the actual break-in. Also, he stated that some of the dogs were confined to a given room or tied up in the house and as a result, would not have been able to investigate the disturbance. He logically assumed that the dog should have barked up a storm, but none did.

He told me that they had thought that possibly a sound device was being used to distract the dog during the break-ins. So he purchased a silent dog whistle and went to some of the homes during the day to see what would happen if he was blowing it while he approached the house. He said that by the time he reached the house he was so out of breath that when the people answered the door, he couldn't talk and he had to sit down. Then, while sitting there, he tried blowing the whistle. In each case, every dog barked. One dog hid under a table, but it did continue to bark.

He then contacted an electronics expert to discuss the possibility that a sound device could be used automatically to immobilize the dogs and people. He also asked me what I thought. My own feelings were that sound would not keep a dog quiet. If anything, it should cause them to bark more or at least get very nervous. I based that statement on tests I conducted a few years back for a government investigation. So he said, what did I think, shouldn't these dogs bark at the sounds in the night? Of course I told him that I would assume they would. He then wanted to know if there was any way that I knew of to accomplish keeping a dog quiet before entering a home. Now that was a very interesting question.

After thinking it over, I could only think of one way to accomplish this task. I said that the average person would take or let their dog outside before going to bed at night. It would seem conceivable that it would be possible to place in the victim's yard, a piece of liver sausage or something similar that contained a tranquilizer or sleeping pill. Then after the lights in the house went out, the burglar could check and see if the bait had been eaten by the dog. The pill would take a while before it took effect and the dog, out of sheer habit, would be wherever he would normally be by the time it took effect. If so, it would be safe to assume that by 2:00 a.m. the dog would be sound asleep. The detective felt that made sense and it was worth looking into.

I told him that in all cases of problem solving with dogs that I encounter, the best way to find the source of the problem is to recreate the situation, make our observations and then proceed accordingly. I suggested that it would be interesting to recreate some of the robberies. I felt that in doing so, we could observe the dog's reaction.

69

It would seem that if we were to recreate the robberies between 2:00 a.m. and 5:00 a.m. and in the process of
doing so the dog at least barked at us, we could then
safely assume that the dog had been drugged the night of
the actual robbery. The detective thought it was a good
idea, but that he would have to okay it with the captain
first. Only a short time passed before he called me back.
The captain liked the theory and idea. He said he had the
permission to contact six of the victims and request they
cooperate with our experiment. I felt that to achieve the
desired effect the people should not be told on what night
we would be coming around. We had to have the scene as
close as possible to how it was the night of the robberies, so the following arrangements for the voluntary homes
were made.

The victims were told that sometime in the next five
days we would recreate the robbery and would they all
sleep in the same places and make sure their dog was in
the same area he was on the night of the robbery. The
detective called back two days later and said all arrangements were made and asked if I could meet him at 1:00 a.m.
the next morning. I agreed.

The night of our experiment was cold, about 5° above
zero, with no wind. I met with the detective in his office where he explained the details of the case. He looked as tired as me, for he originally worked the day shift.
He showed me the pin map and it clearly showed that the
robberies were confined to one part of town. He then
showed me the profile chart that also showed how similar
each robbery was. He gave me a stack of reports on each
case and started pointing out the facts that each contained concerning the dogs in the house.

Sure enough, an interesting pattern was obvious. Not
once did the dog or people wake up no matter what method
was used to break in. Sometimes a door or window would be
pried open, usually with a tool taken from a garage. At
other times, believe it or not, a window would actually be
broken in order to gain entrance. Again, not once did a
dog sound an alarm.

He explained to me many other interesting facts such

70

as how for the most part, only money was taken. Usually
a purse was taken and the next day, the purse would always
be found nearby, placed on a porch. It was obvious the
burglar wanted it returned. He was only after the cash.
They had many sets of fingerprints, but so far they did
not help.

At 2:30 a.m. we went out on the street. We were in
a plain car. The squad cars in the area were informed
that we were going out, but no more information was given
that could be heard over the radio because of the possibility of someone listening in on a police scanner radio.
It was weird to realize that while we were going to imi-
tate being the burglar, odds were the real burglar was in
the area also.

We agreed that we would park a half block away from
the first home and proceed on foot. We both admitted to
being a bit nervous for while it was true the residents of
the house knew it was us and so did the patrol cars, the
neighbors didn't. Needless to say, the people in the area
had become uptight.

The detective put his badge on the outside of his
coat and carried a walkie-talkie. We got out of the car
at our first stop. It was so quiet I swear you could hear
a pin drop. We quietly closed the car doors and proceeded
to the first house. There was a slight crust of snow on
the ground and because it was so still and cold, it was
impossible to approach quietly. We sounded like a herd of
elephants. We approached a large two-story house from the
side and made our way to the rear door. The front of the
house was lit up by a street light, but the rear was pitch
black. Entry had been made in this case by opening an un-
locked rear porch door and then by breaking the glass in
the rear door in order to get in. The dog, a schnauzer,
was loose in the downstairs area. We walked up the rear
steps and opened the porch door (a metal one) which made
a lot of noise. We began to knock and then bang on the
rear doors. The noise we made was at least as much as
would be needed to break in. As soon as we did that we
took note of any and all responses to our noise. We observed the dog's reaction, the people's reaction and the
neighbors' reaction — especially the neighbors, for we

71

had no desire of being shot as a prowler. You could not see the detective's badge in the dark. We made our observations and went back to the car.

At the next house, we proceeded in the same way, but we noticed that someone was still awake. We decided to go to the rear door anyway and knock on it just to observe the dog's reaction. We did so and when the owner came to the door we identified ourselves. We made a note of the dog's reaction and went back to the car.

At the third house, we could not see an address. Not wanting to go to the wrong house, the detective started to head for the neighboring house where a light was on in order to check on the address. The house was set back from the street about 300 feet. As he approached up the front walk, he made a lot of crunching noise while walking. A large dog was in a pen outside and at the first sound of the footsteps, the dog started barking. The detective returned and said we were at the right spot so we proceeded to the victimized house.

In this case, entry was made from a side window at the brightest spot of the house. The glass and sill still showed signs of the fingerprint dust. We started banging on the glass. We noticed that the neighbor's dog, who was now only about 75 feet away in his pen, did not bark at us even though he did when we approached from the front. We made our noise, made our notes and then moved on. By now, we were getting the feel of this prowler business, but we were also getting very cold.

At the fourth house, entry was made from a front window adjacent to an enclosed porch. The family dog was being kept on the porch the night of the robbery. He was there on the night of our arrival also. We made noise and made note of the reactions. By now, we knew what to expect. When we got back to the car, we also decided to see what would happen if we drove into the driveway with the lights on. We did so and then opened the car door to hear if that would alert the owners or their dog. We made our notes.

At the fifth house, entry was made by breaking a side

72

window. In the process, several flower pots on the inside were knocked over. This house had two full grown dobermans. As we approached the side of the lit up house, we could read a large sign on the gate. It said, "CAUTION - MEAN, VICIOUS DOGS - DO NOT ENTER". The report said the dogs were in the house the night of the robbery. We hoped the people did what they were supposed to do and have them inside this week. We tried to open the gate, but it was stuck. So we pounded and kicked it, but it wouldn't open. Apparently the same had happened to the burglar. Not being able to get into the backyard is what probably prompted him to enter from the side window. A light was on so we could observe what was taking place as a result of the commotion we were making. A neighbor's light was also on, so we kept an eye over our shoulder just in case. Our observations were duly noted.

At the last house, entry was made by prying open some patio doors on a rear deck. We noticed that the neighboring house was still awake. We could see the TV on. We made our way to the rear and proceeded with our, by now, familiar routine. The bedrooms were right above us and the dog was loose in the house. We made our notes.

The time was now 3:30 a.m. The detective radioed in that we were finished. The dispatcher asked how it went. The detective's reply was, "I'll tell you about it when I get in. You won't believe it."

Before heading in, we did a little patrol duty riding up and down the side streets with the car lights off. The detective said it was a very standard procedure. He did spot someone walking the streets. I didn't see him. He jumped out of the car and questioned him, for it was strange to find someone walking that late at night, especially since it was so cold out.

As far as the results of the experiment went, a definite pattern surfaced. Surprising as it may seem, <u>not once</u> were we detected by the residents of the house. <u>Not once</u> did a neighbor spot us and last but not least, no matter what we did, <u>not once did the dog in the house bark at us.</u>

This, of course, blew my mind. I had to try one more test. I, myself, keep four dogs in the house; three retrievers and a shelty. I know my dogs and there was no way that they wouldn't bark under the same circumstances. I have been told by numerous people that have come over when we are not home, that they feared the dogs would come through the window at them. They couldn't believe how vicious they could act when being protective. I have also noticed that when we come home late at night, the sound of four dogs can be heard way before we reach the door.

Once, two years ago, we had to go out of town. When we do, we have a couple come in to watch the house and care for the kennel. He had to work late that night, but we had to leave early. When they arrived that evening (we were gone by then), they were unable to enter the house. The dogs wouldn't let them in. They spent the night in a motel. The next morning everything was okay. The dogs let them in, but not at night. Yes, I know my dogs, they would at least bark.

So here it was 4:30 a.m. One more test. My house. I live in the country and it is very quiet. I approached the house from the side and banged on a window. I walked around the house and made noise at all five sliding glass doors. I then entered the house. One dog was in the kitchen; one dog was with my son; two dogs were with my wife. I made noise in the house, but not a bark could be heard. I looked into one of the bedrooms and there, sound asleep, were two of my great watch dogs. The dog in the kitchen was also still asleep. Not only did the dogs sleep through the noise, but so did my wife and teenage sons.

Never having had the opportunity to conduct this type of experiment before, at first I was a bit flabbergasted. But then after giving it much thought, it all became clear. It is now quite obvious to me why the dogs did not react in the expected way. Of course, it is my own theory, but I feel sure that I am right. I believe you will find my answer is logical and, surprisingly, shocking.

Here is what I believe 90 percent of dog owners are inadvertantly doing. Put yourself in this scene. It is

74

a quiet night, but windy. A branch of a tree is knocking against the house or some other noise is occurring due to the wind. Your new, young dog hears these sounds and barks. But you, knowing it is only the wind, shouts at the dog to be quiet. Or, suppose a neighbor comes home late at night and the sound of the car in the driveway causes your dog to bark. Again, you tell him to shut up and so on. On and on it goes; your dog barks at a new noise in the night and you, knowing the source of the noise, proceed to quiet the dog. In time, due to repetitious training procedures, you will <u>probably</u> end up teaching your dog <u>not</u> to bark at noises in the night.

It is important for you to realize that a dog is a pack animal by nature and he will instinctively comply with the wishes of the pack leader. If you have the proper rapport with your dog, you should hold the distinction of being the leader. I call it being a controlling force. What happens, then, is this. Every night, 365 days a year, approximately eight hours a day, one-third of the dog's life, you are teaching him to rely on you. You are teaching him that you are in charge and you are the controlling force. As a result, at night when you are sleeping, you become the motivation, the controlling force that insists and commands a "no bark" rule. Now, if you are out for the evening and the dog is home alone, he would probably bark at various noises in the night. The pack leader is gone, the controlling force has been removed and the dog, responding to standard survival instincts, will act accordingly.

Let me point out an example. To those of you that have traveled with your dog and have stayed in a motel, can you remember the first couple of times? Your dog is quiet at night at home, but you get very upset in the motel because he barks at new, unfamiliar noises that he hears. You immediately tell the dog to shut up. In a very short time, you will become successful in teaching your dog to rely on you to sound the alarm. Once again, you have taught your dog <u>not</u> to bark at sounds in the night. You reaffirm the fact that you are in charge. Yes, you are the controlling force. A dog is a creature of habit. They will do what they have done before when placed in the same situation.

The scarey part of all this is that you are probably just like me. You have heard or noticed as I have, that your dog or dogs are doing a fine job of guarding your home when you aren't there. But you have not realized that you are commanding your dog to accept the fact when you climb into bed for the night, that you are now in charge. You sleep soundly, feeling secure that if there is trouble, your dog will let you know. Yet, not realizing it, your dog is doing exactly the same thing. He is sleeping soundly, content that you, the controlling force will sound the alarm.

We have trained and programmed our dogs to behave in this manner. We have spent more time teaching this response than ony other thing. Every night, over and over, we teach "Don't bark!", "Be quiet!", "I'm in charge!".

I'm sure you're curious as to how your own dog would respond. So I suggest that you try the test yourself. Remember, in order to get the proper results, you must totally recreate the scene. You and all of your family must be in bed as usual. Because of different stages of sleep, I suggest the hours between 2:00 a.m. and 5:00 a.m. Also, you should not be aware of what night the test is going to take place. If you did know, you wouldn't sleep as sound as normal. You would not drift into the normal stages of sleep yourself and, as a result, your dog may not act normal. This, of course, is an inconvenient test to make, but I think you will find the results surprising.

As it turns out, for what it is worth, it is safer to break into an occupied house than it would be to break into a house where the owners are out for the evening.

Good night and pleasant dreams ZZZZZZZZZZZZZ.

16. CLOSING REMARKS

This book has been presented to you as an educational experience. With it, I have attempted to implant some insight of animal behavior and modification in you.

The simplicity of the animal mind can, at times, be a very bewildering and perplexing experience to a human being. Hopefully, I have been successful in modifying your behavior and insight; for if I have, I can be absolutely certain that I have been equally successful in accomplishing the same with your pet.

So, in reality, we cannot call this the end - we must call it --------------- THE BEGINNING.

17. REVIEWS AND COMMENTS ON BOOK ONE

TRAINING A DOG TO LIVE IN YOUR HOME
BOOK ONE: HOUSEBREAKING - CHEWING

"The book's eighty-three pages are filled with line-drawing illustrations and a writing style that is clear and complete. It explains the difference between discipline and punishment, so dog owners can enjoy their pets more. For obedience trainers, this book can help reinforce information which you are conveying to your students."

> Boarderline Magazine
> January/February 1981
> American Boarding Kennels Assoc.

"Mr. Weiss gives sound advice on preventing problems, emphasizing the need to motivate the dog to make the correct decision rather than control him in every situation. I would not hesitate to recommend this book. I look forward to seeing what Mr. Weiss' succeeding books will bring."

> Fran Ennis
> OFF-LEAD Magazine
> March 1981

"As the author notes, this book does not consume much time to read, but whatever time spent is worthwhile. The diagrams in this text are very clear and thus useful. This is another reason for buying the text. However, if the most-hard-to-please individual cannot find one, let him examine the captivating drawings by Joyce Bond. These alone makes the book worth the time and money expended. Personally, I look forward to Book II."

Dr. Beverlee A. Smith
Assistant Professor
Dept. of English & Philosophy
Purdue University (Hammond)

"I think the book is excellent! It definitely fills a need that no other book does, to my knowledge. And I have an extensive dog library."

Sidney Mihls
New Rochelle, New York

John D. Weiss *Proudly Presents . . .*

A Complete Hometraining Program for You and Your Dog

Training A Dog
To Live In Your Home

BOOK ONE:

ISBN: 0-960-4576-0 (1980)

Do these problems concern you?

* HOUSEBREAKING
* CHEWING
* JUMPING ON PEOPLE
* FOOD STEALING
* BARKING
* GARBAGE STEALING
* RUNNING AWAY

DO YOU KNOW . . .

--- Just what housebreaking means? (Do you really understand?)

--- Paper training is <u>not</u> the way to housebreak your puppy?

--- Why he does that? (Learn how to see situations from a dog's point of view.)

--- 85% to 90% of all problems encountered by dog owners are a direct result of the mistakes the owner made while trying to housebreak a puppy?

--- Preventing problems is easier and better than trying to solve them later?

--- Odds are he <u>won't</u> "grow out of it"?

It doesn't just happen. Everyone wants a well-mannered dog – a dog that you can trust in your home – a dog that doesn't need to be constantly watched and scolded – tied up because he runs away – locked in a room when you have guests because he can't behave – in short, a dog you can enjoy and be proud of. One _you_ control.

You _can_ have a dog you can be proud of – a dog you control – but, remember, your dog can only learn to be as good as you make him. It takes more than love and good intentions to raise a dog. IT TAKES KNOWLEDGE – knowledge of the proper way to raise a puppy. TRAINING A DOG TO LIVE IN YOUR HOME will take you step-by-step through those first crucial months of owning a dog. It has been written not just for new puppy owners, but for owners of dogs of all ages.

TRAINING A DOG TO LIVE IN YOUR HOME contains 84 pages packed with information to guide any concerned dog owner on the path of successful dog ownership. There are 21 charming illustrations by Joyce Bond. TRAINING A DOG TO LIVE IN YOUR HOME is written by John D. Weiss, a professional trainer best known for his use of applied psychology to dog training. It is the result of years of study and hours of observation of dogs and dog owners.

TRAINING A DOG TO LIVE IN YOUR HOME – "BOOK ONE"

is clear, easy to read and IT WORKS!!!

ANIMAL OWNERS MOTIVATION PROGRAMS
P. O. BOX 16
FRANKFORT, ILLINOIS 60423

PRICE – $6.95 (plus 75¢ postage & handling) Illinois residents add 36¢ sales tax per book

CANADIAN RESIDENTS Please remit in American funds

Cover Design and Assistance:
Tom and Pat Watanabe

On front cover:
John D. Weiss

Ch. Sun Dance's Ringmaster, C.D.X.
(Golden Retriever)